HARRY & LARRY'S EPIC ADVENTURE

The Copernicus Chronicle

Written by Tracey O'Brien · Pictures by Dayne Sislen

Five Principles Press

Copyright © This Edition 2021
Five Principles Press
St. Louis, MO

Text copyright: © 2021, 2017, 2014 by Tracey Oakes O'Brien
Illustrations copyright © 2021 by Dayne Sislen
All rights reserved.

First Published in the United States by Five Principles Press
Library of Congress Control Number: 2021917664
Printed in USA
ISBN 978 1 7373257-1-0

Dedication

To Nick and Matt, my two explorers who are the inspiration for the characters, Harry and Larry. Be courageous enough to go after your dreams!

It was one of those days.
We were stuck in our room.
We were wild, even beastly,
Because of the gloom.

While the tracks for our trains
Lay strewn on the floor,
I kicked soccer balls
At the goal by the door.

It had rained for days.
The black clouds still loomed.
Winds howled and trees moaned
As thunderclaps boomed.

We each chose to laugh
At the storm and the rain,
Unaware as eyes peered
Through our windowpane.

A sound at the window,
A rush of cold air,
Made us both wonder,
What could be lurking there?

When a long, pointy claw
Reached in through the crack,
Our window flew up.
It leaped in with a smack.

It was furry and soaked.
Water dripped to the floor.
We each backed away,
Ready to bolt for the door.

But his cheerful voice called,
"I like soccer a lot."
So we passed him a ball,
And he gave it a shot.

He was fast on his feet
And quite good as goalie.
At the end of our game,
Here's the tale he told me.

His name was Aldo.
He had seeds that were rare.
He showed them to us,
Then gave Harry the pair.

"They're moving," said Harry.
I saw the seeds bounce in his hand.
"They have power," said Aldo.
"I'll help you to understand."

Shaking water from his fur,
He warned us, "Beware.
There's a seed-stealing squirrel
Called Tom who's out there."

Can seeds have power?
My brain was in a whirl
As I asked about Tom,
The surly squirrel.

Harry, who was now dripping,
Yelled over the thunder,
"Do squirrels wear jackets?"
His eyes were wide with wonder.

"You have many good questions."
Aldo laughed. "That's true.
You're kind and you're curious.
Your mind's open, too."

Then he made us an offer
That changed our whole day.
If we helped him, he'd show us
A new game to play:

A daring adventure,
And, most of all, fun—
A magical game
To intrigue anyone.

"Awesome!" We nodded,
Asking, "What do you need?"
"A jacket," he said,
"Would be helpful, indeed."

We cut Harry's slicker
So that it would fit.
With two strips of duct tape,
We completed it.

Beaming, he hugged us.
He placed a seed in his claw.
Wriggling vines filled our room.
I stood watching in awe.

EARTH SCIENCE

We climbed on a vine.
We swung up and around.
We spotted a man
And then jumped to the ground.

"He looks odd," Aldo said.
"He lived long ago.
There's a story here
That I'd like you to know.

Nicolaus Copernicus
Was this man's name.
His radical ideas
Earned him great fame.

Though he had studied math,
Astronomy, and law,
It was math and the stars
He had loved best of all.

Without telescopes,
He saw the planets and sun,
Measuring distances between
The sun and each one.

ASTRONOMY

But the math made him wonder.
Did it prove something new?
Does the sun circle the Earth?
No, that could not be true.

The sun is the center.
The planets go around.
The calculations prove it.
The model is sound.

His discovery made many
Question his work.
They all laughed at him.
While others called him berserk!

Back then they believed
The planets and the sun
Revolved around Earth.
So thought everyone.

But he didn't give up.
He wrote a book
And invited others
To take a look.

He taught us to learn
And to do what we ought,
To believe in ourselves,
When others do not."

When Aldo stopped talking,
We heard a click.
A seed sprouted up
With speed that was quick.

"A young seed." Aldo jumped.
"So exciting and new!
No new seeds have been seen
For a decade or two!

By learning, you've earned this seed.
So you get to decide
Whether to pursue the knowledge
That's waiting inside.

Tom will want all the seeds.
He doesn't want you to know
How to ask questions,
To think on your own, and to grow."

"But why," Harry asked,
"Would Tom take what's ours?"
"Fear," he replied.
"Knowledge gives you powers."

Then a shadow crept near,
And a snarl filled the air.
"Pick the seed," Aldo warned,
Whisking us out of there.

We tumbled through the air,
Harry next to my side.
But the seed, was it lost?
Had it been cast aside?

We landed in our room
And opened our eyes.
The seed plopped on Harry,
Much to our surprise.

"This seed is for both of you.
You know what to do.
To learn is to create dreams.
Let's plant it, you two!

Dreams are whispers of the heart,
Of what's yet to be.
Open your minds to learn
From those you meet and see."

Safe in our room,
I held the seeds in my hand.
Aldo said he'd be back.
He left while we planned.

In the dark Harry asked,
"What should we do?"
"Plant it," I said.
"It's for me and for you."

We drifted off to sleep.
I felt bold and elated.
While outside in the dark,
A squirrel sat and waited.

www.ingramcontent.com/pod-product-compliance
Lightning Source LLC
Chambersburg PA
CBHW061128170426
43209CB00014B/1702